my

DIVA

journal

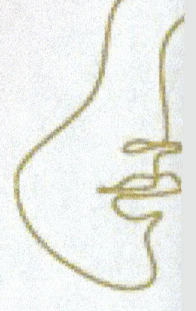

© 2025 L.J.Kulow. All rights reserved.

How to Use My DIVA Journal

Complete one journal page each day—that's it! Each day includes:

A 'Pause & reflect' Question – Explore yourself and your growth by answering the question for the day. This practice helps you witness your own transformation, uncover patterns, and deepen your self-awareness. There are no right or wrong answers—only honest ones. Let your thoughts flow freely onto the page. Some days you'll write more, other days, a single sentence. Both are perfect. If answering a question is too much, just use the space to reflect on how you are feeling and how you would like to feel.

A Practice of Your Choice - Browse the list of practices at the back of your journal and choose one that feels right for today. These simple practices help you build sustainable, nourishing habits. Pick what calls to you and remember to add it to your 'wins' section.

Your Wins - This is where the magic happens! Celebrate everything: getting out of bed, something that went right, saying no when you meant no! Small wins build momentum for bigger ones. On hard days, sometimes the win is simply getting through it—and that absolutely counts. Remember: completing your journal page is always a win!

Your Intention for Tomorrow - Keep it simple and achievable. This isn't a rigid commitment—it's a gentle direction, a soft focus for the day ahead. And here's the beautiful part: you can always change course. Flexibility is part of healing.

Remember: This journal is your supportive companion, not your taskmaster. Be kind to yourself as you fill these pages. You are doing amazing.

 Use the tick box to keep track! Colour/draw in and around it, or just pop a tick in it.

My DIVA Journal

Welcome to your personal companion on the journey to rediscovering your inner *DIVA*.

I've created this journal as a companion to the *DV to DIVA* book. It is more than just a place to write—it's a sacred space for your transformation. Within these pages, you'll discover daily affirmations to rewire your thinking, guided exercises to reconnect you with yourself, inspiring practices to elevate your energy, and room for honest reflection and journaling.

This journal is designed to keep you accountable to yourself with the loving consistency that real change requires. It's your anchor when distractions call, your gentle guide when the path feels unclear, and your witness as you reclaim yourself one day at a time.

When you complete your journal, simply reach for another or use a notebook of your choice and continue your journey using the practices and reflections provided.

Each day flows through the four pillars of the DV to DIVA framework—Divine, Intelligent, Vibrant, and Authentic— a companion that walks alongside the *DV to DIVA* book. This isn't just about reading and learning; it's about living, creating and becoming.

Important note

This journal is a tool for personal reflection and growth, not a replacement for professional therapy, medical care, or other support services. Please continue to work with qualified professionals and maintain your support networks as part of your healing journey.

Day 1 — I am Divine

"I am not broken. I am breaking through to the divine strength that is always within me."

♡ **Pause & reflect** - What does "divine protection" mean to you personally, and where have you already experienced it on your journey?

_____
_____
_____
_____
_____
_____
_____
_____
_____
_____

♡ **Daily Practice — today I choose** _____

♡ **Todays Wins**

_____
_____
_____
_____

♡ **Tomorrows Intention:**

_____
_____
_____
_____

Day 2 — I am Intelligent

"I am intelligent enough to recognize my own worth."

♡ **Pause & reflect** - Whose opinions have you been measuring yourself against? What would change if you released that measurement?

_____
_____
_____
_____
_____
_____
_____
_____

♡ **Daily Practice** — today I choose _____

♡ **Todays Wins**

_____
_____
_____

♡ **Tomorrows Intention**

_____
_____
_____

Day 3 — I am Vibrant

"My genuine self is beautiful, whole, and enough."

♡ Pause & reflect - What activities or people drain your energy? What boundaries might protect your vibrancy?

_____
_____
_____
_____
_____
_____
_____
_____
_____

♡ Daily Practice — today I choose _____

♡ Todays Wins

_____
_____
_____
_____

♡ Tomorrows Intention

_____
_____
_____
_____

Day 4 — I am Authentic

"I am safe to be my true self."

♡ **Pause & reflect** - When do you find it hardest to be authentic? What fear is underneath that difficulty?

_____
_____
_____
_____
_____
_____
_____
_____
_____

♡ Daily Practice — today I choose _____

♡ Todays Wins

_____
_____
_____
_____

♡ Tomorrows Intention

_____
_____
_____
_____

Day 5 — I am Divine

"I am open to receiving divine guidance and inspiration."

♡ **Pause & reflect** - How do you currently connect with your source/higher power? What practices make you feel most spiritually aligned?

_____
_____
_____
_____
_____
_____
_____
_____
_____

♡ **Daily Practice** — today I choose _____

♡ **Todays Wins**

_____
_____
_____

♡ **Tomorrows Intention**

_____
_____
_____

Day 6 — I am Intelligent

" I trust my mind's ability to learn, grow, and adapt."

♡ **Pause & reflect** - How has your emotional intelligence grown through different experiences? What can you see about yourself now that you couldn't before?

_____
_____
_____
_____
_____
_____
_____
_____
_____
_____

♡ **Daily Practice** — today I choose _____

♡ **Todays Wins**

_____
_____
_____
_____

♡ **Tomorrows Intention:**

_____
_____
_____
_____

Day 7 — I am Vibrant

" I am radiating positive energy that attracts good things into my life."

♡ **Pause & reflect** - What passion or joy have you been neglecting? How might you begin to reclaim it?

_____
_____
_____
_____
_____
_____
_____
_____
_____
_____

♡ **Daily Practice** — today I choose _____

♡ **Todays Wins**

_____
_____
_____
_____

♡ **Tomorrows Intention:**

_____
_____
_____

WEEKLY CELEBRATION!!

Each word you write is an act of reclaiming yourself. You are

brave!

You've done 7 days of journalling and practice.

WELL DONE!

Day 8 — I am Authentic

" I release shame and embrace my authentic story."

♡ **Pause & reflect** - What does "showing up honestly" mean in your daily life? Where are you already doing this?

_____
_____
_____
_____
_____
_____
_____
_____
_____

♡ **Daily Practice** — today I choose _____

♡ **Todays Wins**

_____
_____
_____
_____

♡ **Tomorrows Intention:**

_____
_____
_____
_____

Day 9 — I am Divine

" I am worthy of love, peace, and abundance simply because I exist."

♡ **Pause & reflect** - What would trusting the process look like in your life today? What fears come up when you consider letting go?

___

♡ Daily Practice — today I choose ___

♡ Todays Wins

___

♡ Tomorrows Intention:

___

Day 10 — I am Intelligent

" I make choices that honour my wellbeing and future."

♡ **Pause & reflect** - What valuable lesson did you find in a difficult experience? What would it take to see the blessing in our experiences?

_____
_____
_____
_____
_____
_____
_____
_____
_____
_____

♡ Daily Practice — today I choose _____

♡ Todays Wins

_____
_____
_____

♡ Tomorrows Intention:

_____
_____
_____

Day 11 — I am Vibrant

"My energy is returning, stronger and brighter each day."

♡ **Pause & reflect** - What would it feel like to speak your truth with both courage and compassion. How would you feel?

♡ **Daily Practice** — today I choose _____

♡ **Todays Wins**

♡ **Tomorrows Intention:**

Day 12 — I am Authentic

" I honour my true feelings without judging them or hiding them."

♡ **Pause & reflect** - What would it feel like to speak your truth with both courage and compassion. How would you feel?

_____
_____
_____
_____
_____
_____
_____
_____
_____
_____

♡ **Daily Practice** — today I choose _____

♡ **Todays Wins**

_____
_____
_____
_____

♡ **Tomorrows Intention:**

_____
_____
_____

Day 13 — I am Divine

" I am never alone. I am always supported."

♡ **Pause & reflect** — In what ways do you feel supported. What other supports could be available that you haven't thought of yet?

_____
_____
_____
_____
_____
_____
_____
_____
_____
_____

♡ **Daily Practice** — today I choose _____

♡ **Todays Wins**

_____
_____
_____
_____

♡ **Tomorrows Intention:**

_____
_____
_____

Day 14 — I am Intelligent

" I trust that everything is always working out for me."

♡ **Pause & reflect** — What's possible here? Reflect on some of the infinite positive or miraculous possibilities and soften into them.

_____
_____
_____
_____
_____
_____
_____
_____
_____
_____

♡ **Daily Practice** — today I choose _____

♡ **Todays Wins**

_____
_____
_____
_____

♡ **Tomorrows Intention:**

_____
_____
_____

WEEKLY

CELEBRATION!!

You are not what happened to you. You are how you rise.

You've done another 7 days of journalling and practice.

AMAZING!!

Day 15 — I am Vibrant

"My energy levels reflect the love I give myself."

♡ **Pause & reflect** - What movement brings you joy? How can you add more of that joyful movement into your daily life or routine?

_____
_____
_____
_____
_____
_____
_____
_____
_____

♡ Daily Practice — today I choose _____

♡ Todays Wins

_____
_____
_____

♡ Tomorrows Intention:

_____
_____
_____

Day 16 — I am Authentic

"I am practicing distinguishing my true inner voice from internalised criticism."

♡ **Pause & reflect** — How does it feel in your body when you listen to your true inner voice? How does it feel in your body when you hear criticism or negative self-talk?

_____
_____
_____
_____
_____
_____
_____
_____
_____

♡ **Daily Practice** — today I choose _____

♡ **Todays Wins**

_____
_____
_____
_____

♡ **Tomorrows Intention:**

_____
_____
_____

Day 17 — I am Divine

" I release anything that no longer serves my highest good."

♡ **Pause & reflect** – What story, belief, scenario or thought are you holding onto right now that you might be ready to surrender?

_____
_____
_____
_____
_____
_____
_____
_____
_____

♡ **Daily Practice** — today I choose _____

♡ **Todays Wins**

_____
_____
_____

♡ **Tomorrows Intention:**

_____
_____
_____

Day 18 — I am Intelligent

" I have the wisdom to set boundaries that protect my peace."

♡ **Pause & reflect** — What new boundaries could you put in place to look after yourself? What would it feel like to embody the essence of a strong, bold and beautiful woman?

_____
_____
_____
_____
_____
_____
_____
_____
_____

♡ **Daily Practice** — today I choose _____

♡ **Todays Wins**

_____
_____
_____
_____

♡ **Tomorrows Intention:**

_____
_____
_____

Day 19 — I am Vibrant

" I choose vitality over exhaustion, joy over resignation."

♡ **Pause & reflect** — When do you feel most alive and vibrant? What elements are present in those moments?

_____
_____
_____
_____
_____
_____
_____
_____
_____

♡ **Daily Practice** — today I choose _____

♡ **Todays Wins**

_____
_____
_____
_____

♡ **Tomorrows Intention:**

_____
_____
_____

Day 20 — I am Authentic

" I am learning to show up authentically, releasing the habit of being someone I'm not to appease or impress others."

♡ **Pause & reflect** — Reflect on the times you felt the need to hide yourself. What do you do differently now?

_____
_____
_____
_____
_____
_____
_____
_____
_____

♡ **Daily Practice** — today I choose _____

♡ **Todays Wins**

_____
_____
_____
_____

♡ **Tomorrows Intention:**

_____
_____
_____

Day 21 — I am Divine

" The universe conspires in my favour."

♡ **Pause & reflect** — What would it be like to live each day knowing things are always working out for you, and that you just need to allow? How could you practice the art of allowing?

_____
_____
_____
_____
_____
_____
_____
_____
_____
_____

♡ **Daily Practice** — today I choose _____

♡ **Todays Wins**

_____
_____
_____
_____

♡ **Tomorrows Intention:**

_____
_____
_____
_____

WEEKLY CELEBRATION!!

You are discovering who you are beyond the pain. That person is beautiful.

You've completed 21 days of journalling and practice.

GO YOU!!

Day 22 — I am Divine

" I am a sacred being always deserving of love and respect."

♡ **Pause & reflect** — As many times as you can today, repeat quietly to yourself "I am always loved and respected". Reflect on what was different today and how it changed the way people around you behaved.

_____
_____
_____
_____
_____
_____
_____
_____
_____
_____

♡ **Daily Practice** — today I choose _____

♡ **Todays Wins**

_____
_____
_____
_____

♡ **Tomorrows Intention:**

_____
_____
_____
_____

Day 23 — I am Intelligent

" I have the intelligence and intuition to recognise when something isn't right "

♡ **Pause & reflect** — Reflect on a time when your intuition shone through, and you made good decisions based on the guidance of your inner wisdom.

_____
_____
_____
_____
_____
_____
_____
_____
_____

♡ **Daily Practice** — today I choose _____

♡ **Todays Wins**

_____
_____
_____
_____

♡ **Tomorrows Intention:**

_____
_____
_____

Day 24 — I am Vibrant

" I am reclaiming my zest for life."

♡ **Pause & reflect** — How does your body communicate its needs to you? When do you listen, and when do you override those messages?

_____
_____
_____
_____
_____
_____
_____
_____
_____

♡ **Daily Practice** — today I choose _____

♡ **Todays Wins**

_____
_____
_____
_____

♡ **Tomorrows Intention:**

_____
_____
_____

Day 25 — I am Authentic

" My authentic expression is a gift to the world."

♡ **Pause & reflect** — What gift do you have that you can share with the world? What gift would you love to have to share with the world?

_____
_____
_____
_____
_____
_____
_____
_____
_____

♡ **Daily Practice** — today I choose _____

♡ **Todays Wins**

_____
_____
_____

♡ **Tomorrows Intention:**

_____
_____
_____

Day 26 — I am Divine

" My spirit is unbreakable, no matter what I've endured."

♡ **Pause & reflect** — If you could hear a message from your higher power right now, what do you imagine it would say about who you are and the strength you've shown?

_____
_____
_____
_____
_____
_____
_____
_____

♡ **Daily Practice** — today I choose _____

♡ **Todays Wins**

_____
_____
_____
_____

♡ **Tomorrows Intention:**

_____
_____
_____

Day 27 — I am Intelligent

"I honour both my logical mind and my intuitive knowing."

♡ **Pause & reflect** — Describe a decision you made recently using your judgment and intuition. What did trusting yourself in that moment teach you about your intelligence and capability?

_____
_____
_____
_____
_____
_____
_____
_____
_____
_____
_____

♡ **Daily Practice** — today I choose _____

♡ **Todays Wins**

_____
_____
_____
_____

♡ **Tomorrows Intention:**

_____
_____
_____
_____

Day 28 — I am Vibrant

"I radiate positive energy that attracts good things into my life."

♡ **Pause & reflect** — When was the last time you felt genuinely joyful or playful? What would it take to invite more of those moments into your life, even in small ways?

_____
_____
_____
_____
_____
_____
_____
_____
_____

♡ **Daily Practice** — today I choose _____

♡ **Todays Wins**

_____
_____
_____
_____

♡ **Tomorrows Intention:**

_____
_____
_____
_____

Day 29 — I am Authentic

"I give myself permission to change, grow, and evolve."

♡ **Pause & reflect** — How has your definition of "enough" changed? What makes you whole and beautiful today?

_____
_____
_____
_____
_____
_____
_____
_____
_____

♡ **Daily Practice** — today I choose _____

♡ **Todays Wins**

_____
_____
_____
_____

♡ **Tomorrows Intention:**

_____
_____
_____
_____

Day 30 — I am Divine, Intelligent, Vibrant & Authentic

" I have come so far and I honour myself and my unique journey."

♡ **Pause & reflect** – Describe a moment where you felt all four of these aspects, Divine, Intelligent, Vibrant and Authentic working together in harmony.?

_____
_____
_____
_____
_____
_____
_____
_____
_____

♡ **Daily Practice** — today I choose _____

♡ **Todays Wins**

_____
_____
_____
_____

♡ **Tomorrows Intention:**

_____
_____
_____

MONTHLY CELEBRATION!!

One month of choosing yourself, your truth, and your healing.

You are a warrior, and this is just the beginning.

WELL DONE! YOU ARE WORTH CELEBRATING!!

Daily Practices

Each of these daily practices helps build a new mindset and new habits. Each is very powerful on its own or used in combination with each other. Some appear incredibly simple, but when we stop, breathe, and connect with the divine, we access the power that lies in the simplicity of life and the universe. I myself dismissed some of these practices in my early journey from DV to DIVA, but once I learned the power within them, I integrated them easily into my everyday life. They are not just practices, but a way of living that supports us in incredible ways.

Awareness practice

This is a simple and powerful exercise that I use throughout my life still. Simply say to yourself as many times a day as you remember, "I am aware". Write it on a sticky note on your bathroom mirror, by the tea kettle or in your office space. This powerful phrase will help increase your awareness and becoming aware opens you to infinite possibilities. You will notice yourself becoming more aware of your feelings, other people's energies, the energies around you. You will become more aware of the divine nature that is you and become aware of small shifts in your life. You will become aware of when you are tensing, when you feel 'heavy' or when you are feeling lighter and more at ease. Becoming aware allows you to choose in any moment the frequency you want to focus your attention on.

Mirror Practice

Stand in front of a mirror and speak to yourself as you would to a beloved friend. Start with simple affirmations like "Hello (your name), you are worthy."

This can be a little confronting if you haven't done it before. And as with any affirmation, if it doesn't ring true, try softening it a little. Instead of going straight for "Hello (your name), I love you and admire you. You are strong and Beautiful!", maybe start gently "Hello (your name), I see you".

It is important not to resist the resistance though. Gently notice what resistance comes up, this shows you where your vibration needs healing attention. If you are struggling with telling yourself you are beautiful, and there is a tightening in the body, just look at yourself and say "It's ok that I feel this way". Start with a smaller part of the body to love and appreciate that doesn't have an emotional charge. It could be that your hair looks nice today. "Hello (your name), your hair looks lovely today".

Each time you pass your reflection, get into the habit of quickly thinking to yourself or saying out loud, "hello lovely!" or something nice that you might say to someone you love.

The first time I decided to speak to myself in the mirror, I took one look at the broken lady in the reflection, and I cried and cried. I called it ugly cry, cos it sure wasn't pretty! It was so hard, I felt even less beautiful, and the words would not come out. I literally started by saying "Hi," and then looking away.

Now I look in the mirror at home, the reflection of the car door, shop windows or mirrors and I can almost give my reflection a high five. I say "Hi beautiful", and I can usually feel that I look amazing! This exercise is powerful and works.

Three-way alignment meditation

This meditation brings your three intelligence centres—your brain, heart, and gut—into rhythmic alignment. When these centres synchronize through slow, intentional focus on the heart and breath, you shift from stress and scattered thinking into an aligned state of calm, clarity, and deeper intuition.

1. Slow the breath. Breathe in through the nose for 5 seconds and out through the mouth for 7-8 seconds. This reminds the body it is safe. Do this for a minute or two, keeping your rhythm slow and consistent.

2. Place a hand over the centre of your chest. Feel your heartbeat. I like to use my fingertips on my sternum. Place your attention on your heart, the feeling of it beating and at the same time focus on breathing slowly and deeply.

3. As you breathe in, imagine the breath is love, light and appreciation flowing into your heart. You can say the words "love" or "thank you".

4. As you breathe out, imagine you are breathing love, light and appreciation out of your heart and into every cell in your body.

5. Stay in this meditation for 5-10 minutes, whatever feels comfortable, ensuring your attention is on your heart while focusing on the breath. If your attention wanders, gently bring it back.

6. You can stop here if you like or while in this state you can ask a question. You have access to your divine intelligence and intuition from this space. Some answers may come later, some immediately. Either way is fine but ensure you don't try too hard. Soften into the process, trust it and allow.

Daily Empowerment Tapping Practice

You may choose to do a rating on this one if you don't feel empowered. Otherwise, just enjoy this empowering practice!

Karate Chop - repeat 3 times while tapping - choose one, rotate all three, or choose your own specific statement.

"I choose to start this day connected to my power"

"I honour myself and my journey today"

"I am worthy of all good things coming to me today"

Round 1: Grounding in the Present

EB - I am here in this moment now

SE - I honour where I am today even if I feel a little off, it's all ok

UE - I release yesterday's struggles

UN - I don't need to think about tomorrow

CH - Right now, in this moment, I am safe

CB - In this moment, I breathe in peace

UA - I am centred and calm

CR - I am present here and now and I am ok

Round 2: Opening to Possibility

- KC – What if I can be open to infinite positive possibilities?
- EB - I'm open to what today brings
- SE - I trust myself to handle whatever comes
- UE - I'm worthy of good things happening
- UN - Opening to joy, peace, and ease
- CH - I allow life to support me
- CB - I'm open to unexpected blessings
- UA - I trust in the unfolding of this day
- CR - I'm ready for, and deserving, positive experiences

Round 3: Empowerment

- KC – What if I really am powerful and capable?
- EB - I trust myself completely
- SE - I am worthy of love, joy, and peace
- UE - I am Divine, Intelligent, Vibrant, and Authentic
- UN - I am aligned with my highest good
- CH - I am exactly where I need to be right now
- CB - I am enough, right now, as I am
- UA - I choose empowerment in every moment
- CR - I am a DIVA! Divine, intelligent, vibrant and authentic

The A+ instant reset

This simple technique is powerful in any moment of high emotion, fear or illness. Every time something comes up in your body feel into it and allow it to release so you can experience calm and ease and allow something different.

Use in moments of exploration, overwhelm, fear, not knowing what to do, anxiety, physical illness.

1. <u>Acknowledge</u> - You are aware that you are feeling off, feeling fear or feeling dis-ease in your body. Acknowledge that. Listen to the body for a moment. Feel into the emotions. Allow the feelings to be there, no matter how intense. Don't be afraid if they intensify while you are acknowledging them. Tell your body "I am aware, I feel you body, thank you body for protecting me, thank you for this communication". Rate the discomfort on a scale of 1 – 10 and be totally ok with it.

2. <u>Air</u> – Your reminder to breathe into it. Regardless of if you feel heightened or you feel like you don't need to calm down, take a moment to relax into your current feeling. It's ok that I am feeling this. It's ok that I am here now with this happening. Breathe in through the nose for 5 seconds, pause, breathe out like you are gently blowing a candle out for 7-8 seconds. Pause your breath before breathing in again. Breath deep into the belly allowing it to expand and allow the belly to sink in as your release the breath. Do this 3 times.

3. <u>Allow</u> – When you acknowledge the feelings in your body (step 1) this allows for a transmutation of the energy. Rather than resisting, shoving it down, ignoring it, you acknowledge it to allow the shift. By breathing (Step 2) you have calmed your nervous system. From this place of acknowledgement and calm, you can now allow something different. There are two ways to do this.

<u>Ask</u>; how does it get better than this? what would it take for…? what is possible here?

Or,

<u>Affirm</u>; I am allowing peace in my body now, I am allowing something new, I choose to feel calm, I am stronger than this moment, I am moving through this.

Quick version of The A+ instant reset.

A – Acknowledge the feelings. I am feeling _____ in my body.

A – Air – your reminder to breathe. In for five, out for eight, three times.

A – Allow something different using Ask or Affirm – What's the best that can happen? I am moving through this experience.

Identifying and changing Beliefs exercise

A belief is a thought we feel in our body to be true. And some of the beliefs we carry—the ones we absorbed from family, society, past trauma—are lies that our bodies have learned to accept as fact. When we live through these beliefs, our life is limited. Example,

Belief: money is hard to come by.

Limit: not enough money.

This exercise will help you identify those limiting beliefs, understand where they came from, and begin the process of releasing them.

You'll Need: A quiet space where you won't be interrupted, Paper and pen & 20-30 minutes.

Before you start take three deep, aware belly breaths, in for the count of 5, out for the count of 8. Allow the belly to expand on the in breath and deflate on the out breath.

Step 1: Identify a limiting belief - Ask, "what limiting beliefs are active in my body right now?" or try these prompts.

"I am not enough because..."

"I can't have/do/be because..."

"Other people see me as not enough because..."

Don't filter or judge what comes up. Write quickly. Let the beliefs flow onto the page, even if they seem silly or contradictory. Examples might include:

- "I am not enough because I'm not married"
- "I am not enough because I don't earn six figures"
- "I am not enough because I'm not thin enough"

Step 2: Find the Root - Look at your list. Circle the beliefs that feel the most charged—the ones that make your chest tighten or your stomach drop. Pick your top three.

For each one, ask: *"Where did I learn this? Who taught me this was true?"*

Write down the memories, people, or moments that come to mind.

Step 3: Challenge the Belief - For each circled belief, answer these questions:

- Is this true for me?

- What evidence do I have that contradicts this belief?

- Would I say this to my best friend if she believed it about herself?

- Who benefits from me believing this about myself?

Step 4: Rewrite the Truth - For each limiting belief, write a new truth. Make it present tense, personal, and powerful.

Old belief: "I am not enough because I'm not married" *New truth:* "I am whole and complete exactly as I am. My worth exists independent of any relationship."

Step 5: Release This part is physical and symbolic. Choose one:

- Tear up the page with your old beliefs and throw it away (or burn it safely)

- Cross out each limiting belief with a thick black marker

- Write your new truths on a fresh page and place it somewhere you'll see daily

- Or simply say out loud, "I now release this old belief".

Moving Forward: These beliefs didn't form overnight, and they won't disappear overnight either. When an old belief surfaces (and it will), acknowledge it: "There's that old story again." Then consciously choose your new truth instead. With practice, your body will begin to feel the new truth just as deeply as it once felt the old lie.

www.ingramcontent.com/pod-product-compliance
Lightning Source LLC
Chambersburg PA
CBHW060531010526
44110CB00052B/2560

9780975653654